Redpolls, Twites & Linnets

Peter Lander and Bob Partridge
Photographs by Dennis Avon MIOP ARPS

(Popular British Birds in Aviculture: No 3)

Redpolls, Twites & Linnets

Peter Lander and Bob Partridge

KINGDOM

Published by Kingdom Books
PO Box 15
Waterlooville PO7 6BQ
England

Contents

Preface

This book is the third in a series intended as a follow-on to the very successful book *British Birds in Aviculture*, published in conjunction with the British Bird Council. By concentrating on no more than three species in each book we can treat them in much greater depth. It also enables us to update the original book where necessary in the light of the latest knowledge and experience.

Our old friend the late Walter Lewis always used to say, 'The golden rule in bird breeding is that there is no golden rule.' By this he meant that there are always exceptions in anything to do with birds, and the experience of one successful breeder is totally different to that of another, for no apparent reason. Walter was considered to be one of the most knowledgeable British fanciers of his time in the field of British birds, mules and hybrids.

All we can do is pass on our knowledge and experience as a basis on which each breeder can develop his or her own system. As joint authors we can sometimes give different information, hopefully making this book all the more interesting and useful.

Peter Lander, Bob Partridge

Popular British Birds in Aviculture series:

No 1: Greenfinches   *No 2: Siskins and Goldfinches*

No 3: Redpolls, Twites and Linnets   *No 4: Bullfinches, Chaffinches and Bramblings*

Cages and Aviaries

Before obtaining any birds it is essential to have suitable accommodation. While this need be neither expensive nor ornamental, it must be suitable for the birds' needs. They must have room to move about freely, shelter from the elements and protection from enemies such as cats, owls, weasels, rats and other vermin. There must also be sufficient food and water receptacles.

Birds certainly look better in an aviary but, for enthusiasts who have neither the space nor the means, adequate accommodation can be provided in cages. These can be situated in a shed in the garden. However, many sheds need extra windows to allow the birds enough light to feed throughout the day - if the shed is dark they will spend a lot of time roosting. There must be good ventilation, allowing continuous free passage of air. Heating is not necessary for temperate-zone birds normally resident in this country throughout the year. On the other hand, it is essential that the birds can drink at all times during the day and, unless the fancier is at home all day, the shed should be heated or insulated sufficiently to prevent the water from freezing during severe weather. A study of the advertisements in the fancy press will produce information on sheds in a variety of shapes and sizes, all designed for bird keeping.

Birds need room if they are to breed - in fact the larger the cage the better. The minimum size recommended is 91cm (36in) long by 60cm (24in) high by 46cm (18in) back to front, containing only one pair. Far better results will be obtained by having a few pairs in large cages than by having more pairs in smaller cages. Natural branches can be fixed in the cages for perches; these look nicer and are much more comfortable for the birds' feet than the round doweling often used, but do not overcrowd the cage with these as flying space is essential. In one end of the cage fix a bunch of conifer or other suitable evergreen, with a forked branch in the middle to support a nest. Alternatively a small wicker basket or half-open-fronted, open-topped box can be used (fig 1). The object is to provide privacy and a feeling of security for the sitting hen, but the bunch must not be thick enough to exclude too much light or prevent the birds from entering easily: just enough to give the necessary seclusion.

Contrary to advice frequently given, the most consistent results are obtained in sheds and aviaries facing east. This is because birds, particularly when nesting, do not like being

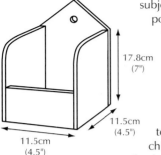

17.8cm
(7")

11.5cm
(4.5")

11.5cm
(4.5")

Fig 1: Nesting box

subjected to the mid-day sun and, in the wild, nearly always choose a shaded position. They also like protection from the prevailing west winds and, in the wild, choose a situation that is protected in this respect also. It is not always possible to provide the ideal so it is advisable to fix up some means of providing shade and protection.

The only real disadvantage to cage breeding is the extra work involved in providing a sufficient variety of foods on which the birds can feed their young, particularly when they are first hatched. Even in a small aviary it is much easier to provide a variety of foods, and the birds will find a few insects to supplement their diet, which can be so beneficial in the early stages of a chick's life. To some extent this can be overcome if the birds can be persuaded to feed the young ones on egg food. More details on feeding are given in chapters 5 and 9.

It is not essential to provide near-natural conditions to breed our popular native birds. The majority of these common species can be reproduced with the minimum of cover in a small flight. Even a large cage will suffice for many of the hardbills.

Dark yellow linnet mule cock

Some years ago breeders used large amounts of cover in the form of gorse, broom, conifers and other evergreens but nowadays the birds are much more domesticated and breed very successfully with only a minimum of cover. This has the added benefit of allowing the breeder to observe, study and enjoy the birds to a far greater degree.

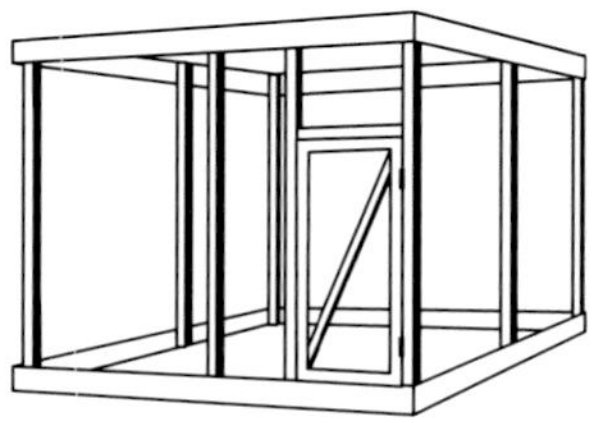

Fig 2: Typical Aviary –
from an original design by Hylton Blythe

Aviary Construction

An aviary can be any size but the minimum recommended is 180cm (6ft) long by 60cm (2ft) wide by 180cm (6ft) high. This will hold approximately six non-breeding birds, but generally only one pair of breeding birds. In a mixed aviary one should allow at least 2.25 cubic metres (80 cubic feet) per pair of birds; much more if possible.

Aviaries can be as simple or as elaborate as one wishes, depending on circumstances and funds available, as long as they meet the requirements of the birds. An example of a cheap and easily-constructed aviary is the one designed some years ago by Mr Hylton Blythe (fig 2), which is made as follows. Roofing laths are driven into the ground at 1m (3ft) intervals and cut off to the required height, with further laths nailed along the top and across from side to side. This enables 1m (3ft) wire netting to be stapled to the laths. There is a small door at one end for access, with a shelf above it for food. A further small door gives access to the shelf so that you do not need to enter the aviary to feed the birds. Cover must be provided to keep the seed and shelf dry. The birds also need protection from the wind and rain and shade from the sun. This can be achieved by nailing boards all along the top to a width of about 30cm (12in) and the same along the top of the sides. Roofing felt can be used instead of boards if there is wire netting underneath to support it. If all the timber is treated with creosote or bitumen it will last much longer.

Where funds allow, more substantial aviaries give added protection to the birds and last considerably longer. A well-constructed and well-maintained aviary can more than repay the extra expense and labour. For example, solid foundation plinths set well into the ground constructed of 10cm (4in) bricks, blocks or solid concrete 45cm (14in) deep will keep out rats. The base area can then be filled in with earth, pebbles, sand, bark chippings or solid concrete or slabs for easy cleaning and disinfecting. Tanalised framing or cedar wood 50mm x 50mm (2in x 2in) will last almost a life time.

Solid timber felted roofs give valuable protection from cats, kestrels, marauding magpies and thunderstorms and also exclude droppings from wild birds, which can pass on disease to the aviary inmates. Solid cladding of the back and at least one third of the sides gives added protection as well as security to the birds (fig 3).

Large feeding trays can be provided in a completely dry area where they are clear of any perches, thus preventing the birds from eating mouldy or soiled foods. These and many other refinements can be considered for the welfare of the birds, which is paramount if success is to be achieved.

For nesting sites, use small wickerwork baskets with a few twigs tacked around. This gives the birds some degree of privacy. Even so, many birds pick nesting sites completely open to view, despite other more secluded sites being available. Two or three sites should be available to each pair of birds. Provide a little extra cover for any particularly shy specimens. Other acceptable nesting sites are square wooden pans with perforated zinc bottoms. These are used by many breeders of canaries. Canary plastic pans will need to have felt linings glued or sewn inside, but the birds often pull these to pieces, leaving the slippery plastic surface on which they cannot shape a nest. However, a little polyfilla or plaster of Paris wiped roughly around the inside can be helpful. Plywood or cane strawberry punnets or clay flower pots can also be used. Sites and receptacles will depend on what the birds find acceptable.

Any simple structure with suitably-sized netting will keep birds in, but it is much more difficult to keep vermin out. Some refinements have already been mentioned to overcome this but, if you do not intend to have solid plinths and solid roofs, other methods have to be used. Cats can be a nuisance, especially if they get on the top of an aviary. To overcome this the main frame should be extended about 23cm (9in) and this extension covered with 5cm (2in) netting, often called chicken wire. Cats have difficulty in walking on this netting, and bunches

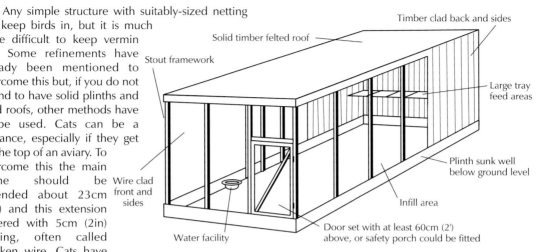

Fig 3: A well constructed aviary 1.8m x 3.6m x 1.8m (6ft x 12ft x 6ft) would accommodate 4 mixed pairs or up to 20 non-breeding birds

of gorse hung facing downwards on the corner posts will deter them from climbing up.

Rats, if they gain access, kill the birds and drag them down their holes. This can be overcome by digging a trench round the aviary 30cm (12in) deep and 30cm (12in) wide. The wire netting is extended down the side of the trench and along the bottom in the shape of a letter L. The trench is then filled in.

Mice are much more difficult to exclude. Although they do not kill birds directly, they carry diseases and cause considerable disturbance, jeopardising breeding results. Also, where mice can get in, weasels will follow, and they kill and eat every bird in sight in no time at all. Mice and weasels can get through 1.3cm (0.5in) netting which is generally used for aviaries: 1cm (0.375in) netting, which is much more expensive, will keep out all but baby mice. It is therefore very important to keep a sharp look out and take quick action if any signs of mice are seen, by setting traps and putting down poison. Both traps and poison must be suitably protected

from pets and children, especially as they generally cannot be placed inside the aviary. However, there are now some traps which catch the mice alive and can be used inside an aviary safely.

A small aviary for each pair of birds is considered ideal, especially if you intend to specialise in a particular species. On the other hand, large aviaries containing several species, such as pairs of redpolls, siskins, linnets, twites and goldfinches, will

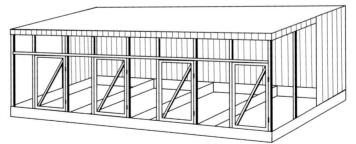

Fig 4: A similar sized aviary partitioned to take 4 segregated breeding pairs; a front corridor could be added for safety

prove perfectly satisfactory. Greenfinches can usually be trusted with these smaller finches throughout the year, and can also be housed with finches of their own size, such as bullfinches, chaffinches, bramblings or buntings,

Isolated Type of Nesting Site

a: Basket wired to
stout twigs

b: Surrounded by evergreen
twigs and wire-tied

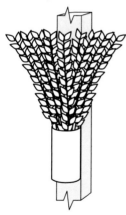

c: Finished nesting site
inserted in down-pipe
which has been fixed
to framework

Fig 5: Nesting sites

outside the breeding season, though it is not recommended that these species are mixed during the breeding season. Housing of all species needs careful consideration to suit individual needs.

Trouble can be experienced when just two pairs of different species are kept and bred in one aviary, because one pair will sometimes chase the other continually, preventing feeding. It is best to have either one pair or three or more pairs in a flight. This usually prevents the trouble, but always provide a large feeding area or several smaller ones.

The pros and cons of different materials for the floor area, touched on earlier, are really governed by the conditions and needs of both the birds and the keeper. Earth is the natural floor covering and, provided that overstocking is avoided, the birds can derive much benefit in the form of trace elements from the soil. Waste seeds which germinate are a welcome addition to the birds' diet. The vegetation attracts a myriad of insect life, which again is very beneficial, especially when young are being reared. The drawback is that it is difficult to prevent mice from burrowing in and breeding in the aviary, contaminating both the food and the soil. Earth floors are also difficult to disinfect and keep clean. Liming annually helps keep it sweet, but the soil will undoubtedly need renewing completely to a depth of 15cm (6in) every few years if problems with disease are to be avoided. Small washed pebbles laid to a depth of 10-15cm (4-6in) are a good alternative. Seeds still germinate and the birds derive benefit from searching amongst the pebbles. Mice will not take up residence if a good depth of loose pebbles is maintained. Pebbles can easily be riddled to remove waste, washed and disinfected.

Forest bark chippings on an earth floor can look very attractive and again discourage mice if a good covering is maintained. The bark should be about 8-10cm (3-4in) deep and must be raked over now and again to freshen it up. It must also be removed and replenished occasionally. Spent bark can be composted and used in the garden.

Concrete is sterile and stark and can be cold and damp during inclement weather, but the dampness can be almost eliminated by laying plastic sheeting down before concreting. A layer of sand on top of the finished floor will take away the starkness. It has the advantage of being easy to clean and disinfect and is rodent-proof.

Solid wood floors are also worth considering, having similar benefits to concrete, but being much warmer. However, this type of floor will need to be raised some 30cm (12in) above the ground, allowing a good air flow beneath it to prevent rotting and stop rodents from gaining access. The whole structure can be set on stilts such as concrete pillars or blocks and bricks with plenty of ventilation holes.

We now come to furnishing the aviary. Most hardbills (and redpolls, twites and linnets are no exceptions) quickly defoliate any living plants and shrubs. Most will not survive such treatment for long, although vegetation such as elderberry, blackberry and stinging nettles sometimes survives if the aviary is not over-populated. The aviary should be furnished with natural branches such as willow, ash, elder, hazel, apple or pear. These should be located sparsely and high up, providing safe perching and roosting places but still leaving plenty of space for flying exercise.

Since growing shrubs are not usually practical when you are keeping hardbills, substitutes must be provided. There are various ways of doing this using evergreen branches from the conifer tree family. Where single pairs are housed, a couple of isolated nesting sites will be adequate. These are made by wiring a few short branches or twigs of the chosen evergreen around a wickerwork basket or some other similar receptacle (fig 5). For most birds these should be fixed fairly high, close to the roof. Short lengths of gutter down pipe (approximately 15cm (6in) of 6.5cm (2.5in) diameter) screwed to the framework in suitable places as nesting sites can easily be fixed and replaced as required. Where several pairs are housed together at least two such sites must be provided for each pair. They can also be made a little more substantial to give each pair more privacy. This helps avoid the odd skirmish of pairs guarding territory.

Many breeders find the hedge system by far the most satisfactory. Strange to say, a continuous hedge all down one side or the back seems to overcome territorial problems, and pairs nest close to each other without any fighting. The artificial hedge is built in the following way. Vertical spacers about 5cm (2in) thick are fastened to the side of the aviary. Then laths are nailed horizontally about 25cm (10in) apart, starting from the top. It is not necessary to go below about 75cm (30in) from the floor. If possible, choose the west or south-west side. If the outside of this part of the aviary is of wood, or some other solid material, so much the better. If not, cover it with hessian or roofing felt to provide protection and privacy. Bare, forked branches are now placed in the laths to simulate the inside of a hedge.

After this, conifer branches or other evergreens such as heather and gorse are threaded into the laths producing a finish rather like an uncut hedge. It is important that this should not be too thick and that there are holes in the foliage through which the birds can obtain access to the inside of the hedge where they will build their nests. Do not forget to put a covering 30–46cm (12–18in) wide on the outside of the aviary over the top of the hedge to provide shade from the sun and shelter from the rain.

If birds are to be kept in a very open aviary all the year round, it is best to attach some sort of shelter shed to it so that the feeding can take place inside, and it may be necessary sometimes to confine the birds inside as well. The shelter shed can be as large or small as you desire, or it can be the main bird room with the aviary built on the side. A container full of grit and a bath of fresh water are other essentials to the aviary.

If the birds are being bred in cages in a shed it is very helpful to have a small flight built on to the end of the shed. The birds are fed inside the shed with a pop-hole to give access to the flight. Young birds, when fully weaned, can be transferred to this flight, leaving the parents free to get on with the next nest. Most birds moult out better in a flight where they have access to fresh air with plenty of exercise and bathing facilities.

It is recommended that all birds be ringed, and it is worth bearing this point in mind when deciding on the feeding stations. For some pairs it is a great help if the feeding stations can be somewhat obscured from the nesting sites to enable you to ring the chicks unobserved while the parents are feeding.

As previously mentioned, aviaries can be as large or small, as ornamental or heavily-built, as the owner wishes, but all follow the basic pattern of design described and illustrated in the sketches. Refinements can be added according to individual taste.

One point that should be stressed is that it is better not to have the doors too large unless a safety porch is included. If doors are made 90cm–120cm (3–4ft) high and approximately 60cm (2ft) wide an area of 60–90cm (2–3ft) will be left above the door on the usual 2m (6ft) aviary. Birds flying towards the door will go to this space above it as you approach and enter, reducing the possibility of escape. The door should be set well clear of the ground so that it opens and closes freely. Doors can open inwards or outwards to suit the needs of the keeper.

Rambler roses, honeysuckle, clematis, hop and other climbing plants can be grown up the outside of the aviary. They look very attractive and help to attract greenfly and other insects from which the birds will benefit. However, the growth must not be allowed to interfere with the general maintenance of the aviary. If the growth penetrates the wire netting for a prolonged period it can create holes that are large enough to allow birds to escape. This can easily happen before the damage is noticed by the keeper.

Chapter 2

Evolution

We now come to a group of species that in the past were assigned to a separate genus, *Acanthis*, but are now rightly included by scientists in the genus *Carduelis*. Redpolls, twites and linnets are all very similar in appearance and lifestyle, being very closely related, but have evolved to take advantage of three entirely different habitats. The **redpoll** is a bird of the northern birch forests and the tundra, the **twite** is a mountain bird inhabiting upland moorlands, and the **linnet** is confined to lowland heath and scrub.

There are no similar birds in South America or South Africa, but the linnet breeds along the north-west African Mediterranean coast, throughout Turkey and along the coast of Israel. Northern and eastern races tend to be paler and less heavily streaked than western region races. There are two close relatives, evidently populations which have become isolated at some time:

- The Yemen linnet *(Carduelis yemenensis)* breeds along the Red Sea coast. It differs from the linnet in having a greyer head, a broad white wing bar and chestnut on the wing-coverts, lacking the red on the forehead and the streaking on the breast.
- The Warsangli linnet *(Carduelis johannis)* is confined to Northern Somalia. It is mainly grey with little streaking.

The twite's breeding range extends eastwards from Europe into Turkey, parts of central Asia and China. Again, eastern races tend to be paler and less heavily streaked, race *montanella* being the palest.

Redpolls breed along the Arctic Circle right round the world: Scandinavia, Russia, Siberia, Alaska, Canada, Greenland and Iceland. They are closely related to siskins, which they resemble in many ways, but the yellow ground colour has been lost except for on an area of the forehead and, to some extent, on the breast and rump, where their natural foods bring out a red or pink flush, especially in males in breeding condition. The linnet and the twite are also white-ground birds, but in the linnet any red or pink areas are confined to forehead and breast. In the twite there is no red on head or breast, the pink flush being confined to the rump.

It is generally accepted by leading authorities that there are four species and at least three sub-species:

- The lesser redpoll *(Carduelis flammea cabaret)*. This is the smallest of the redpolls, nutty brown in colour with darker streaking. The richest coloured in this group are from the most westerly areas of its European range.

- The 'common' mealy redpoll *(Carduelis flammea flammea)*. This is a greyer-coloured, larger bird. The more northern specimens tend to be larger and lighter-coloured. The sub-species 'Holboll's' *(Carduelis flammea holboelli)* is a larger, longer bird, with longer bill and large bib.
- The Greenland redpoll *(Carduelis flammea rostrata)* is considered to be the largest, and is darker in colour than the other races, with heavy streaking. The sub-species *(Carduelis flammea Icelandica)* is smaller and tends to be greyer in colour.
- The Arctic or hoary redpoll *(Carduelis hornemanni hornemanni)* is a large redpoll, in colour very pale light grey with dark streaking. The streaking can be sparse, and the rump is often devoid of any streaking. The sub-species *(Carduelis hornemanni exilipes)* seems to be somewhere between the Arctic and mealy in both size and colour.

It seems that redpolls, twites and linnets have evolved since the last ice age (about 14,000 years ago) from the same ancestors to take advantage of the three different habitats. Apart from very rare accidental vagrants we only get two species of redpoll in the British Isles: the mealy *(Carduelis flammea flammea)* and the lesser *(Carduelis flammea cabaret).* These are the species covered in the following text, but general care and management are the same for all redpolls.

Agate (silver) mealy redpolls (Right: hen, Left: cock)

Lifestyle in the Wild -
Mealy Redpolls

Order: Passeriforms
Family: Fringillidae (Finches)
Genus: *Carduelis*
Species: *Carduelis flammea flammea*
Common Name: Mealy Redpoll

Description

> Length: 12.5cm (5in)
> Weight: about 14g (less than 0.75oz)
> Wing Span: 17.7cm (7in)
> Tarsus: 1.5cm (0.6in)

Cock

Larger than the lesser redpoll, but crimson of crown brighter, with much paler body. Above it is grey-brown streaked with darker brown. It has a brown, deeply-forked tail, a greyish-white rump with a few dark streaks, a greyish-white stripe over each eye, a blackish bib under its bill, and whitish wing bars. Its tail and wing feathers are edged with pale buff. Pink flush on breast and rump in breeding plumage.

Hen

Same as cock but with more streaks, particularly on the breast and flanks. Does not usually have pink flush on breast or rump. Not an easy bird to sex (see chapter 6).

Juvenile

Similar to hen but more speckled and finely streaked. Almost indiscernible bib, no crimson on the crown, no pink on breast or rump.

Bill

Short, thick and deep at base, tapering sharply to a point. Colour yellow, but browner in the winter.

Legs and Feet

Dark brown, very short legs and comparatively large feet, enabling the bird to feed upside-down when required.

Crop

As with other finches, redpolls have an extendible gullet in which to store food for regurgitation and to help the bird to last through the hours of darkness.

Distribution

The mealy redpoll is circumpolar, breeding right along the Arctic circle, from Scandinavia across Europe, Siberia, Alaska and Northern Canada.

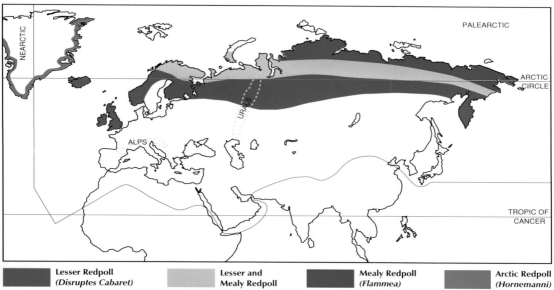

Lesser Redpoll (Disruptes Cabaret)	Lesser and Mealy Redpoll	Mealy Redpoll (Flammea)	Arctic Redpoll (Hornemanni)

Habitat

Northern forests, chiefly birch and alder, or willow-growth on open swamps, or peat mosses. It also breeds in pine forests, but less abundantly.

Migration

When the Arctic winter closes in the mealy redpoll is forced south into central Europe, Central Asia, the United States, Scotland and the east coast of England.

Flight

The typical undulating flight of finches, but rather faster than most, accompanied by continuous twittering.

Lifespan

In the wild they suffer heavy losses in severe weather, when they are unable to feed, and rarely live more than two years. In aviaries they may live longer (see chapter 6).

Main Foods
Tree seeds, especially birch and alder, but they also take many wild plants. In the breeding season, in addition to vegetation and semi-ripe seeds, the young are fed on small insects such as greenfly, particularly in the early stages of rearing.

Flocking
All redpolls are sociable birds, often nesting in loose colonies. In the winter they range far and wide in large flocks, often in the company of other finches, especially siskins, who are also very fond of birch and alder seeds.

Courtship and Territory
In courtship the cock, facing the hen, spreads his tail and flutters his wings above his back, tilting his head back to show his pink breast and black bib. This is often preceded by fast chases through the trees, the cock continuously twittering and trilling. There is also an aerial display in which the cock flies high with a rather bounding flight, calling loudly. Mealy redpolls do not defend much of a territory and frequently nest in loose colonies, feeding in flocks some distance away from the nest.

Mealy redpoll cock

Nesting
Nests are usually built in forks of birch, alder or willow, occasionally in grass tussocks. Nests consist of a foundation of twigs of birch or heather on which are placed such materials as roots, bents and bark fibre. They are then lined with down and feathers or hair.

Eggs
There are usually five or six rather deep blue eggs, their dull surfaces spotted and streaked with light brown. They are rather small.

Laying and Incubation
Being a northern bird, the mealy redpoll does not start laying until the latter part of May, or even early June. Incubation is by the hen alone and starts after the fifth egg has been laid. The cock is often on guard nearby and feeds the hen while she is sitting. There are often two broods. Breeding normally finishes in August.

Young

The young hatch approximately 11 days after the hen starts sitting. They are small, blind and helpless. In the early stages of rearing they are fed by the hen on small caterpillars or small flies but, as they get older, the main foods are seeds of birch, alder and many plants. The cock brings the food to the nest in his crop and feeds the hen, who in turn feeds the young. When the young are about half grown both parents feed them by regurgitation. The hen cleans out the nest for approximately six days, by which time the young are large enough to excrete onto the rim of the nest and their eyes are open.

Fledging

The young leave the nest at approximately 13 days old and the cock will continue to feed them for another 7 to 10 days, after which they join the flock and forage for themselves. Although they are fully feathered when they leave the nest the tail is not fully grown and they may still have tufts of down on their heads.

Knapweed

Moult

The moult is necessary because, after a year, a bird's feathers become worn and are less effective for flight and insulation. In most birds the moult occurs outside the breeding and migration seasons, but while food is still sufficiently plentiful to support the growth of feathers. However, we do not know exactly what brings on the moult. Reducing daylight length has some effect and perhaps colder nights. Nevertheless, not all birds of any given species finish breeding at the same time, although it is not unknown for a pair to commence a late nest, only to abandon it while young are still in the nest and start moulting.

Adult finches replace all their feathers after breeding. Sexual activities cease within a matter of days. The birds become silent and keep mostly in cover. Gonads regress and the sex hormones are replaced by other hormones. The thyroid hormone raises the birds' metabolic rate and controls the growth of new feathers, which are fed from the blood stream, while the skin becomes heavily vascularised instead of being loose and thin.

Feathers are grouped into tracts that run along the length of the body, with bare areas of skin between, as can easily be seen in nestlings. In nestlings, all the feathers grow at the same time until they spread over the whole body. In adults, new feathers emerge in a regular sequence over a period of several weeks. When one feather is grown, the next is shed, so that the bird is never left naked or unable to fly. (Ducks, geese and swans have a different arrangement.) If feathers are knocked out accidentally outside the moulting season, replacement feathers grow immediately, but not if a feather is just broken. Each growing feather is encased in a sheath or quill containing blood. When the feather is about one third grown it breaks the sheath, which shrinks and finally drops away. Within a few days of the feather completing its growth it hardens, the blood supply stops, and it becomes a dead structure held by the muscles at its base.

In adult finches the first feathers to be shed are the innermost primaries and the outermost secondaries of both wings, the last in each wing being the outermost primary and the innermost secondary. The large tail feathers are moulted in pairs, beginning with the central pair. Body feathers are moulted from the centre of each feather tract spreading outwards. In their first moult, juveniles retain their large flight and tail feathers for

Mealy redpoll x linnet hybrid cock

another year. Apart from this they moult their feathers in the same sequence as adults. Most juveniles moult when they are about 12 weeks old, but late-hatched birds moult before that age, when the adults are moulting.

Feathers consist almost exclusively of keratins, which are proteins containing large amounts of sulphur, amino-acids, cystine and methionine. For this reason the birds require a great deal of protein during the moult, which has to come from the food that the birds eat at the time. The true nutritional requirements to provide this are not yet known. The food must be available continuously. Any shortage on even one day is sufficient to cause the formation of a fault bar on the growing feather, which is then liable to break at this point during the year. As well as producing new feathers, the bird loses heat much more easily while moulting and therefore must eat more. Adult mealy redpolls usually begin to moult in September, and the young birds moult into their adult plumage at the same time, but they do not shed their tail or flight feathers until the following year.

Feather Type

In most species, including finches, there are two feather types, and a bird has either one or the other.

- A jonque has shorter, narrow, silky feathers that are much better coloured and make the bird look brighter but smaller. This is generally known by aviculturists as a 'yellow', but this name is very misleading, because it does not refer to the colour of the bird. *Intensive* is perhaps a better term.
- A mealy has longer, broader, coarser feathers, the tips of which are pale buff or white. The bird has a mealy appearance, but looks larger and has a duller appearance than the jonque. This is generally known by aviculturists as a 'buff', but again it is misleading, because it is not connected with the colour of the bird, but with its feather type. *Non-intensive* is a term now frequently used

Both feather types occur in redpolls, but it is not always easy to distinguish between them.

Lifestyle in the Wild -
Lesser Redpolls

Order: Passeriforms
Family: Fringillidae (Finches)
Genus: *Carduelis*
Species: *Carduelis flammea cabaret*
Common Name: Lesser Redpoll

Description
Length: 12cm (4.75in)
Weight: about 12g (less than 0.5oz)
Wing Span: 15cm (6in)
Tarsus: 1.25cm (0.5in)

Cock
Upper parts nutty brown with darker streaks, underparts whitish. Buff coloured bars across the wings, crown crimson, black bib. Rump rosy pink, though usually concealed. Pale line over the eye. Streaked brown on flanks. The short forked tail is dark brown. In breeding condition the cock has a rosy flush on his breast, and this is brighter in birds aged more than a year.

Hen
Very similar to cock, perhaps somewhat fuller and with more streaking on the flanks and into the breast. Does not usually have pink flush on the breast or rump. Not an easy bird to sex (see chapter 6).

Juveniles
Similar to hen, with more dark speckles and streaks on throat and breast, but the bib is almost indiscernible and there is no crimson on the forehead nor pink flush on breast or rump.

Bill
Short and thick at base, tapering sharply to a point. Colour yellow, but browner in the winter, particularly the upper mandible. Short bristle-like feathers at base.

Chapter 4

Legs and Feet
Dark brown, very short legs and comparatively large feet, enabling it to feed upside down when required.

Crop
Lesser redpolls have extendible gullets, known as crops, in which they store food for regurgitation to the young and to help them survive through the long dark nights.

Distribution
The lesser redpoll is resident in England, Wales, Scotland and Ireland, though there is some movement south in bad weather. They are generally rather scarce in Devon and Cornwall. They are also resident in central Europe and Asia to the south of the Arctic Circle. Many move down to the Mediterranean in the winter.

Migration
Flocks arrive from Europe to the east coast of England, from Yorkshire down to Suffolk, from the end of September to the end of October, returning from mid-March to mid-April.

Lesser redpoll distribution in the British Isles (above) and world-wide (below)

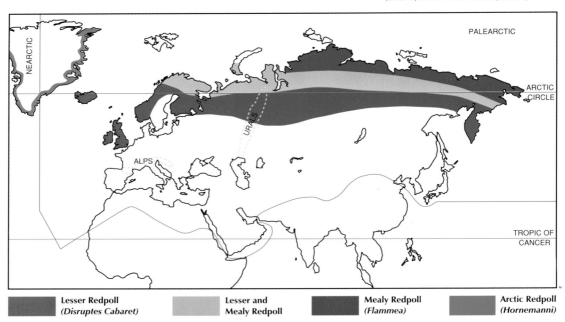

| Lesser Redpoll (Disruptes Cabaret) | Lesser and Mealy Redpoll | Mealy Redpoll (Flammea) | Arctic Redpoll (Hornemanni) |

Flight
Typical undulating flight of the finches, but rather faster than most, accompanied by continuous twittering.

Lifespan
Although several ringed birds aged three or four years have been recorded, there are heavy losses, and few live long enough to breed for more than one season.

Main Foods
Birch, alder, willow for a large part of the year, with minute insects, larvae and their eggs being taken in quantity in the breeding season. They also take chickweed, dandelion, grasses, meadowsweet, willowherbs, bullrushes, persicaria, fat hen, mugwort, tansy and other wild plant vegetation and seeds.

Flocking
Large flocks roam the countryside foraging in winter, often in the company of siskins and sometimes with linnets and other finches. In the summer they continue to feed in flocks, though in smaller numbers.

Courtship and Territory
Redpolls, being sociable birds, do not hold territories like some other species

Cinnamon lesser redpoll cock

and tolerate other members of the species in reasonably close proximity. In courtship display flight the cock flies high in circles, with a somewhat hesitant flight, calling loudly. Afterwards the cock, facing the hen, spreads his tail and flutters his wings above his back, tilting his head back to show his pink breast and black bib.

Nesting
There are generally several nests in close proximity, usually about two to three metres above the ground, though sometimes at considerable heights in high hedges. They can also be found much lower, in short scrub on the outskirts of plantations, young conifers, osier beds, alder swamps and occasionally tall heather. The nest, which is built by the hen with the cock in attendance, has a foundation of thin twigs. It has a roughly-finished external appearance because of the ends of coarse bents and stalks. The lining is down and sometimes hair and feathers.

Redpoll x chaffinch hybrid cock

Eggs
There are usually four or five deep blue, rather small eggs, spotted and streaked with light brown.

Laying and Incubation
Laying usually begins in May, though in the more northerly parts of its range not until June. Incubation is by the hen alone, beginning as soon as the clutch is complete, the hen being fed by the cock. There are usually two broods, sometimes three in the more southerly parts of its range.

Lesser redpoll pair (Left: cock, right: hen)

Young

The young hatch 11–12 days from completion of the clutch, small, blind and helpless. The cock feeds with the flock and fills his crop. Returning to the nest about every half-hour, he feeds the hen with regurgitated food and she then feeds the young. She only leaves the nest for very brief periods for the first few days. After this her absences gradually get longer until about the seventh day, when she ceases to brood the young in the daytime but still continues to brood at night for a time. The hen cleans out the nest, removing all droppings, until about the sixth day, when the young are sufficiently grown to be able to excrete onto the rim of the nest. For the first few days after hatching the cock brings mainly small insects, but he gradually turns more to semi-ripe seeds as the young grow.

Fledging

The young fledge at about 13 days and the cock continues to feed them for another 7 to 10 days, after which they join the flock and are self-supporting.

Moult

Like the parents, the young moult in September, but they do not shed their tails and flight feathers in this first moult.

Feather Type

Jonque (yellow) and mealy (buff) feather types do exist in this species, but they are not always easy to distinguish.

Accommodation and Foods -
Redpolls

ACCOMMODATION

Redpolls can be bred in a cage 2m x 0.5m x 0.5m (6ft x 18in x 18in). They will breed in less roomy accommodation but, since they are very active little birds, anything much smaller would not really be suitable. As with other species, it is a great advantage to be able to shut the parents off in one end while ringing the young birds in the other. Redpolls do not generally go to great lengths to hide their nest, usually building well in view. For this reason they do not need too much cover; a nest pan or wicker basket with a few bits of conifer or other suitable evergreen fastened around it is generally acceptable. Being sociable birds, they can be bred on the colony system (three or four pairs together in a very roomy aviary). This is a help if you are not sure of the sex of each bird; if they have plenty of space, there is very rarely any serious fighting, although they do chase each other about.

The artificial hedge described in chapter 1 is ideal for a colony of redpolls. They can be mixed with other finches in an aviary and rarely cause any trouble. However, it is wise to avoid mixing them with highly territorial species such as bullfinch, chaffinch, brambling or buntings, which can prove pugnacious in the breeding season. Where several pairs, one pair each of several species, are housed in one flight, allow approximately 2.25 cubic metres (80 cubic feet) of space per pair. In such an arrangement good results can usually be obtained. However, best results are undoubtedly obtained when pairs are housed individually.

FOODS

Redpolls are not particularly fussy about their feed but do need a nourishing and varied diet.

Seed

A good basic British finch mixture together with a good condition seed mixture makes a useful staple food, to which can be added a little extra niger seed. The following will also be appreciated:

Hemp: Some hemp will be appreciated, but needs to be limited.

Sunflower: (preferably small striped): Redpolls, like most other finches, enjoy this seed but, like most of the smaller finches, they have difficulty in breaking the husk to extract the kernel. Small quantities should be given in de-husked state (often obtainable from health food stores), or the husk can be split or crushed to give the birds access to the kernel. During the breeding season it can be soaked, after which, if gently squeezed, the softened husk will split, giving easy access to a nutritious feed.

Maw Seed: This is always best fed in a separate pot and is particularly useful when the young are starting to feed themselves or when a bird is a little off colour.

Cinnamon redpoll x siskin hybrid hen

Perilla Seed: This is also much appreciated in small amounts.

Soaked Seeds: Seeds that have been soaked in cold water for 24 hours should be supplied regularly, especially in the breeding season. The water must be changed several times during that period; otherwise the seeds go sour. Rinse well and allow the water to drain off before feeding. A teaspoon of bleach per litre of water kills harmful bacteria and prevents the seed from smelling.

Egg Food

It is important to get the birds used to a good egg food or condition and rearing food similar to that supplied to canaries, and to ensure continuous supplies throughout the breeding season. This is especially important for those being bred in cages, as it is a useful alternative to the insects that redpolls would normally feed to their young. Mixing some soaked seed with the chosen soft food will encourage the birds to take it.

Mealworms

Mealworms provide a suitable animal protein and redpolls take them very readily.

Mealworms are best offered as a daily titbit in the spring, two or three per pair, with soft food. They should be broken or beheaded to immobilise them. The birds do not usually consume the whole mealworm, but extract the contents, leaving the skin.

Do not provide an unlimited supply: too many mealworms can have a detrimental effect on both young and adults, being very high in proteins but lacking in calcium.

Heather

Grit and Charcoal

All seed-eaters should have a clean supply of mineralised grit to help digestion. Small amounts of granulated charcoal can be added to this, as it helps keep the digestive system sweet.

Water

Clean water for drinking and bathing should be supplied daily.

Wild Foods

Wild foods should be supplied as often as possible, though care must be taken to ensure that they have not been contaminated. Chickweed, dandelion, grasses, meadowsweet, fat hen, mugwort, sow and milk thistle, docks and many others will be taken in season.

Supplements

Few additives are needed if a full and varied diet is provided throughout the year. However, some breeders add various supplements to the main foods in an effort to overcome possible shortages, particularly in vitamins and minerals. Care should be taken not to exceed the recommended quantities.

ABIDEC*: This is a very useful vitamin supplement and is best added to the drinking water. There are many other useful multi-vitamin type supplements on the market, any one of which should meet your birds' needs.

Cod Liver Oil: This is a rich source of vitamin D and can be given throughout the breeding season and during the moult. One teaspoonful is mixed thoroughly with one pound of seed, which is allowed to stand for 24 hours before being given to the birds.

PYM*: Yeast can be mixed with seed in almost any quantities, as can mineral mixtures, especially those containing iodine. These are a good help in maintaining healthy condition.

Redpoll mule cock

Tonics: These can be useful, especially the ones containing iron.
Probiotics: These encourage and build up the 'friendly' bacteria whose function is to keep all the 'unfriendly' bacteria in the gut in check. Probiotics can be given daily throughout the year in the drinking water. (Dosage: in accordance with the manufacturer's instructions.)

* Registered Trade Mark

Breeding –

Redpolls

Pairing

As the days grow longer and the temperature rises, less food is required to overcome the cold and the long nights, and there is more time to feed. Consequently the cocks start to come into breeding condition and begin to make overtures to the hens. By the beginning of April, by which time they should have been moved into their breeding areas, the birds should already be paired. If the birds are all left together during the winter they will form their own pairs, which may not be as we would select them. It is better to keep the selected cock and hen together during the winter, allowing them to come into breeding condition together. This way there will be no trouble in pairing the birds as you want them. If you intend to pair the cock to more than one hen, it is best to keep him separate from the hens until required.

Nesting

Redpolls in the wild nest in loose colonies and therefore are easy to breed on the colony system in aviaries (three or four pairs together in one roomy aviary). The artificial hedge described in chapter 1 is excellent for these birds. They like to build their nests on the protruding branches and these are usually in full view. Nests are not as neat as those of some of the other finches, tending to be somewhat bulky. Built on a foundation of small thin twigs, nests consist of bents and stalks, generally lined with down. Supply grass stalks, sisal string cut in short lengths and teased out, or coconut fibre, and dog hair. If seeding dandelions are provided the birds will often use the fluffy down for lining. However, they will just as easily take to constructing a nest in a pan or basket.

Brooding

The eggs are small and rather similar to those of the siskin. Generally, the hen will start sitting when the clutch is complete, but some hens begin from the second or third egg, which can result in chicks hatching at different times and the possibility of losing the late-hatched young. With these hens it may be necessary to foster the smallest chicks to other nests containing young of the same age, or you can replace the first eggs in the clutch with dummy eggs, putting them back when the full clutch has been laid. An incubating hen will only leave the nest for short periods to feed, drink and defecate. The cock will bring her food, feeding her by regurgitation. The eggs hatch in 11-13 days.

Rearing

When the young hatch, blind and helpless, they are fed only by the hen for the first few days. The cock will be looking for tiny insects to feed the hen and, in aviaries, can be seen hanging upside-down on the wire netting collecting gnats and other such food. If the birds are in a cage or in a flight or aviary with no access to natural food plants it is most important to supply as much wild food as possible; the birds will find many small insects on it.

As described in the previous chapter, mealworms are a useful substitute. Most redpolls will take them freely when in breeding condition. Two or three per pair daily in the spring will get them used to them,

Cinnamon linnet mule hen

and the intake should increase to about 30 per pair per day when they have young. You should not provide an unlimited supply of mealworms; they are very high in protein but low in calcium, and too many can have a detrimental effect on the health of the bird. Soaked or sprouted seed is also important, either as an addition or as a substitute for wild food, because after a few days the parents wean the young onto half-ripe seeds.

As the young grow the hen can leave the nest for longer periods and the cock also starts to feed them. The hen cleans out the nest until the young are large enough to defecate onto its rim at about seven days old. At this stage she stops brooding during the day, but will go on brooding at night for a few more days.

At 14 days the young are fully feathered and ready to fledge, although not quite fully grown. The hen may start another nest but the cock will continue to feed the young for about another 10 days, after which they are self-supporting. However, weaning can be a difficult period. Some cocks do not feed the young as they should, or may be required to mate with other hens. If the hen starts to incubate a further clutch of eggs in these circumstances the fledged young may be neglected and will die before they learn to feed themselves. In such cases it is best if the hen is not allowed to incubate a further clutch until the fledged young are independent. This may necessitate removing the eggs. It may be possible to place them under a hen sitting on infertile eggs or a canary to foster. In any event, the hen will usually lay another clutch within 10-14 days, by which time the previous round of young should be fully weaned.

Chapter 6

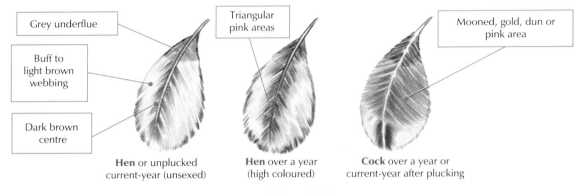

Redpoll breast feathers

Moult

The first young moult into adult plumage at about 12 weeks. Later nests of young moult sooner and later-bred young can moult as early as five weeks. Most retain their flight and tail feathers until the following year. The adults moult between July and September. All feathers are replaced with new ones as described in chapter 3. Feed as many natural foods as possible at this period to bring out the birds' natural colours.

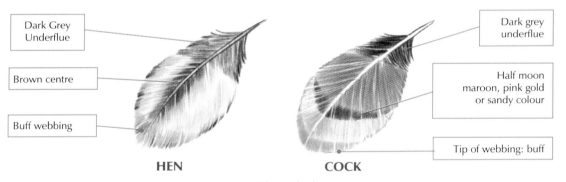

Linnet breast feathers

Colour Feeding

There is no need to colour feed redpolls unless you wish to, but there is no doubt it does enhance their colour. Some of the bigger shows put on classes for colour-fed and non-colour-fed redpolls. This goes back to the time when Spanish red pepper, mixed with egg food, was used to colour feed canaries. Some exhibitors still use this today. Most, however, now use Carophyll Red*, which gives the birds a nice red 'poll' and the cocks a nice pink flush on the breast like in breeding condition, though perhaps a little darker. Carophyll Red* can be administered in food, water or both.

Longevity

Redpolls are prolific breeders in suitable domestic conditions but mortality can be quite high. They seem prone to stress-related illnesses, particularly in their first year, so it is important to avoid conditions that may cause stress. Having said that, individuals reaching ten years of age and more are not unheard of, although three to six years seems general. Twite and linnet youngsters seem more hardy and robust and usually live to a good age, five to ten years being normal.

Sexing

This can be difficult, but it becomes easier with experience. There are certain traits which indicate the sex of a redpoll, such as shape. Hens tend to be fuller or more dumpy looking than cocks and to carry more streaks (striations), usually referred to as 'working', into the chest. Cocks are generally what is termed 'open-chested'. Bibs are usually more distinct in hens than cocks, though in current-year birds the opposite is often the case, young cocks having darker, more defined bibs than hens. The poll colour can also be more distinct in cocks.

All these differences are still only pointers to the bird's sex. However, if the bird is known to be over a year, having undergone at least one full adult moult, then sexing is relatively easy. If the breast feathers are examined closely, cocks will be found to have a distinctly different colouration in this area, showing a mooned effect towards the base of each feather. This area will be dun, gold or pink, depending on the bird's diet during the moult. Birds fed on hard seed only usually show dun or gold colour, whereas those that have been fed on a more natural diet including plenty of wild seeding weeds, or that have had Carophyll Red* added to their diet, display pink mooned areas. Hens do not have this pink mooned area effect in the feather, although some hens (referred to as 'high-coloured') display a pink colouration on the breast, particularly when fed Carophyll Red*. This colouration is situated only in the central webbing of the feather and is triangular in shape.

To sex current-year birds or birds of unknown age showing no moonings, carefully pluck a dozen or so feathers from the upper breast, about 6mm (0.25in) below the bib, with small tweezers. Holding the bird firmly breast uppermost in the hand, remove one or two feathers at a time with a gentle downward pull. Be careful not to tear the skin by removing too many feathers at once. New feathers will regrow in about three weeks and the cocks will show moons on these new feathers. These will be seen much more easily if Carophyll Red* is fed during the period of regrowth; adding it to the water gives excellent results. It is most important that the birds to be plucked have completed their first moult as, if they are plucked too soon, the result is not conclusive. This method of sexing is extremely reliable. Very occasionally there are reports of hens showing cock colouration, but these are extremely rare, usually ageing hens with a hormone disturbance. They are said to have 'struck cock colour'.

Mugwort

Much of the above can be applied to the linnet and twite, which some keepers experience difficulty in sexing. However, there is no need to pluck either of these species, as the cocks will attain colour in their first moult. The linnet cock will show the same mooned effect in the breast feathers as the redpoll. Twite cocks, although showing no 'moons' in the breast feathers, will show similar colouration in the area of the rump, though it will be somewhat darker than that of the redpoll and linnet, being coppery, bronze or plum-red.

* Registered Trademark of Roche Products Limited

Lifestyle in the Wild -
Twites

Order: Passeriforms
Family: Fringillidae (Finches)
Genus: *Carduelis*
Species: *Carduelis flavirostris pipilans*
Common Name: Twite or Mountain Linnet

Description

Length: 13cm (5.25in)
Weight: about 15g (0.75oz)
Wing Span: 19cm (7.5in)
Tarsus: 1.7cm (0.7in)

The continental twite (*Carduelis flavirostris flavirostris*) is like the British twite but generally paler. The following description is for the British twite.

Cock

Does not have the red cap and pink breast of the linnet; otherwise they are similar, the twite being darker and slightly smaller, with a deeper cleft in the tail. White flash on primaries not as obvious as on the linnet. Head and neck streaked black-brown on orange-brown. Upper parts warm brown streaked with dark brown. Breast and flanks buffy orange-brown streaked with dark brown. Belly white-buff. Pinkish rump. Brown-black forked tail, fringed with white on outer webs. In winter, pink on rump much reduced.

Hen

Like cock, but without pink on the rump. Not easy to distinguish in the field.

Juvenile

Just like the hen. Slightly darker upper parts than the juvenile linnet.

Bill

Thick and deep at base, tapering sharply to a point. Nostrils covered by short, bristle-like feathers. Pale yellow in winter, turning to pearl-grey tinged with yellow in the breeding season.

Legs and Feet
Dark-brown, only slightly larger than those of the redpoll.

Crop
Like most finches, the twite has an extendible gullet in which it stores food for feeding the hen and young by regurgitation.

Distribution
In Europe the twite breeds on the west coast of Ireland, in the highlands of Scotland, on the Pennines in England, and on the west coast of Norway and the coast of Lapland. In winter it leaves the high ground and winters on the sea shore on the central west coast of Ireland, some of the western isles of Scotland, the Orkneys, around the Wash and on the Yorkshire and Essex coasts. On the continent, birds that have left Norway and Lapland congregate in large concentrations on the coasts of the Netherlands, Belgium and France. The twite is also found in Turkey and central Asia through to China.

Habitat
Stony mountain moorland and barren, open, windswept environments, including Arctic and Alpine tundras. In winter it moves down to sea coasts.

Migration
The British population only moves down to lower ground along the sea coast, but the Norwegian and Lapland populations migrate south to the east coast of the North Sea.

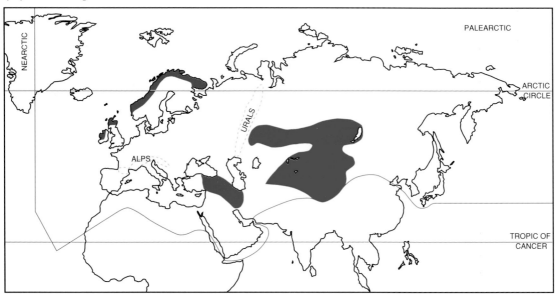

Twite distribution world-wide

Flight
Rather rapid undulating flight, like most finches.

Lifespan
Little recorded information is available, but the average lifespan of the twite must be similar to that of its close relative, the linnet.

Main Foods
Weeds of pasture and cultivated land: dandelions, charlock, wild radish, thistles and hardheads. In winter, sea-aster, marsh samphire, sea-rocket, cord grass, thrift and seablite. Also golden rod, milfoil, mayweeds, marigolds, and mugworts.

Flocking
In winter the twite forages in quite large flocks, sometimes in the company of linnets. In the summer it is more widespread but still a sociable bird.

Courtship and Territory
The only courtship display recorded is the cock repeatedly opening and depressing his wings to display his rosy rump. It is not a territorial bird and breeds almost in colonies with nests often no significant distance apart.

Nesting
Nests, built entirely by the hen with the cock in attendance, are frequently close to or actually on the ground, in long heather, loose stone walls, gorse, among ivy or creepers, under the shelter of an upturned sod and, occasionally, in rabbit holes. The nest consists of grasses, stalks with a few twigs, and some moss, lined with hair, wool and sometimes feathers.

Eggs
There are usually five or six blue or bluish-white eggs with a few bold streaks and spots of very dark red-brown. They are very similar to linnets', but generally bluer.

Laying and Incubation
Laying generally commences at the end of May or early June. Incubation by the hen alone starts when the clutch is complete and lasts for 12–13 days, during which time the hen is fed by the cock. Usually two broods.

Young
The young are fed by both parents by regurgitation on half-ripe weed seeds and some small insects. Seeds include the

Twite distribution in the British Isles

daisy, charlock and dandelion. The young fledge at approximately 15 days and continue to be fed by the parents for a further two weeks.

Moult

Juveniles moult out into adult plumage in the same way as redpolls (see chapter 3) at about 12 weeks. They do not moult their primaries and tail-feathers until their second moult the following year. Late August to September is the time for the adults' annual moult.

Feather Type

This is another species in which both jonque (yellow) and mealy (buff) feather types exist but are sometimes difficult to distinguish.

Twite pair

Lifestyle in the Wild -
Linnets

Order: Passeriforms
Family: Fringillidae (Finches)
Genus: *Carduelis*
Species: *Carduelis cannabina cannabina*
Common Name: Linnet or Brown Linnet

Description
Length: 14.5cm (5.75in)
Weight: 16g (1oz)
Wing Span: 20cm (8in)
Tarsus: 2cm (0.75in)

Cock
Head and neck are streaked blackish-brown and buff with crimson crown, though the amount of crimson varies. Upper parts dullish chestnut with blackish-brown streaks. The linnet does not have a pink rump like the twite. Underparts are buff, with flecks and streaks of dark brown. Flanks are buff, streaked with chestnut-brown. Tail is brown-black with white edging to outer feathers, quite deeply forked. In the wing, seven primaries are edged with white, extending to the shaft. In summer breeding plumage the head and neck turn grey, the upper parts becoming bright chestnut, and there is a pink flush on the breast. A most beautiful bird.

Hen
The hen is the same in both winter and summer, similar to the cock in winter plumage, with only small differences. In the wing, only five primaries are edged with white, and the white only extends to the outer web, not as far as the shaft. The hen has more pronounced streaks on the flanks than the cock. (See also sexing in chapter 6.)

Juvenile
Same as the hen, but without the streaks on chin and throat.

Bill
Thick and deep at base, tapering sharply to a point. Dark brown, changing to steely blue in breeding condition.

Legs and Feet
Dark brown, slightly larger than those of twites and redpolls.

Crop
Like all Cardueline finches the linnet has an extendible gullet, enabling it to store food to be fed to the hen and young by regurgitation.

Distribution
The linnet is widely distributed throughout the British Isles, except on high ground. It was quite numerous but, because changes in agriculture have considerably reduced the weed seeds that are its main foods, its numbers have been greatly reduced and it is now a declining species in Great Britain. It is found throughout central and southern Europe, southern Norway, Finland and the north-west African coast.

Ragwort

Habitat
In summer the linnet frequents gorse-grown commons, young plantations, uncultivated ground with a sprinkling of bushes or scrub and, to a lesser extent, hedgerows and bushy places in cultivated areas. In winter it leaves its summer haunts and moves onto stubble, fallow fields and waste ground, and is frequently found on sea shore and salt marshes.

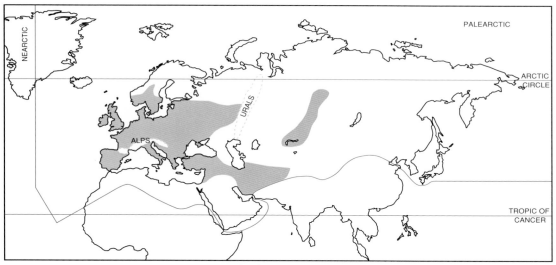

Linnet distribution world-wide

Linnet distribution in the British Isles

Migration

Many British birds move south in the winter, passing through the Netherlands and down through France into the eastern half of Spain. At the same time large numbers of continental birds arrive on the east and south coasts of England. There is reverse migration in the spring.

Flight

Rapid and undulating like that of other finches, generally accompanied by continuous twittering.

Lifespan

Linnets are heavily predated and many nests are lost. Only a small proportion survives to breed and of these birds the average lifespan is about 18 months.

Main Foods

Mainly weed seeds: chickweed, meadow grass, dandelion, Jack-by-the-hedge, sorrel, buttercup, cat's ear, brassicas, thistles, persicaria, fat-hen, mugwort, and meadowsweet. It also takes flax, hemp, turnip and some insects. In addition the young are fed on flies, larvae, small caterpillars and spiders.

Flocking

Linnets flock as soon as the breeding season is over and roam the country in search of seeds, most of which are gathered on or near the ground. They sometimes roost in trees, hedgerows and osier beds, but often on the ground amongst coarse grass.

Courtship and Territory

The cock droops his wings and spreads his tail repeatedly, vibrating the tips of the feathers and singing a sweet low song. Display and coition usually take place on an exposed twig. Linnets are not strongly territorial and usually breed socially with several nests quite close to one another.

Nesting

The nest, built by the hen only, is low down and sometimes actually on the ground, consisting of stalks, bents, moss and sometimes twigs and lined with hair, wool, down or feathers.

Curled dock

Linnet cock

Linnet x bullfinch hybrid cock

Eggs

There are usually four or five pale bluish-white eggs, with spots and occasional streaks of purplish-red.

Laying and Incubation

Laying begins at the end of April or early May. Incubation by the hen commences when the clutch is complete. The cock may relieve her for short periods. Incubation lasts approximately 12 days. There are normally two broods in a season.

Young

The young are born blind and helpless, but soon develop. They are fed on small insects to start with, and weaned onto half-ripe seeds as they grow. Both parents feed them after the first few days.

Fledging

A heavily predated species. The young leave the nest at about 11 days old, before they can fly, and hide in the undergrowth, where the parents continue to feed them until they fledge. The cock will then continue to feed them for about 10 days.

Moult

Like other finches (see chapter 6) the young moult out into adult plumage at about 12 weeks old but do not usually moult the flight and tail feathers until the following year. Late August to September is when most adults moult, the cocks moulting into winter plumage.

Feather Type

In breeding plumage it is fairly easy to distinguish jonque (yellow) cocks, with their brighter and more extensive pink and crimson, from the mealy (buff) individuals. It is a little more difficult to distinguish between the two types in hens and in cocks in winter plumage.

Accommodation and Foods -

Twites and Linnets

ACCOMMODATION

Twites and linnets are timid birds, less likely to breed in cages where they lack privacy. They can be bred in larger aviaries with other species or, better still, in a small aviary on their own. In either case, reasonable cover is needed because the nests are nearly always well concealed.

Although linnets nest low down in the wild and twites on or near the ground, both species will readily accept the type of nesting site recommended for finches in general in chapter 1. A little brushwood can be provided low down for the young to hide in for a few days after they leave the nest, or perhaps a bunch of growing nettles. These would be helpful both for cover and for the insects that the birds use to rear their young. Both species can be termed nervous and leave their nests very easily, usually returning quickly when they feel danger has passed. For this reason, it is best to watch them from a distance to discover where and when they are building. Keep a close watch on the ground for eggshells so that you can estimate when the young hatched and work out the time for ringing, although they will usually tolerate brief, discreet inspections. Both can be mixed with other species of finch, but avoid pugnacious species during the breeding season. In a mixed aviary allow 2.25 cubic metres (80 cubic feet) of space per pair, but in a small aviary on their own the amount of space is not so important as long as the birds feel secure. What is important is that the breeder is able to get in to ring the young birds without the parents dashing about madly. Some provision for shutting the parents off from the nesting area is a great help in small aviaries.

FOODS

Seeds

A good British finch mixture can be used as a basis. Linnets and twites eat more rape seed than other finches, particularly if soaked, but for the best results some extras should be added:

Linseed: These birds are very fond of this, so the mixture should include a good proportion.

Hemp: Another favourite food. Extra can be given in a separate pot, but only in very small amounts.

Niger: This is a thistle, and part of their natural diet in some

Twite cock

areas of their range. If necessary the quantity in the mixture can be increased. This is a very helpful food for bringing the birds into breeding condition.

Maw Seed: This is a great help if a bird is off colour and is also useful when the young start to feed themselves. Being very small, it gets lost in a mixture and is best supplied in a separate pot.

Soaked Seeds: In the wild, birds do not generally eat hard seed, so the provision of soaked or sprouted seed is necessary in the breeding season. When seed is sprouting the vitamin content changes from that in hard seed and it is more like the half-ripe seeds on which the birds feed in the wild. When seed is soaked it is essential to change the water frequently and drain thoroughly.

Dandelion

Egg Food
Birds should always be encouraged to take egg food (as supplied to canaries) because it is high in animal protein, similar to insects, and is a great help in rearing young.

Mealworms
Linnets and twites are not particularly insectivorous, but will seek insects when they have newly-hatched young. Like the redpolls, they will soon learn to take these as a substitute.

Grit
Grit is very important to all seed-eaters and helps the gizzard to grind up the seeds. Good quality mineralised grit for cage birds is recommended.

Cuttlefish Bone
This supplies calcium, which is needed for the egg shells and for the formation of bones in the young. It should always be available, although the birds may not take much of it outside the breeding season.

Water
A fresh supply of clean water for drinking and bathing every day is essential all the year round for the birds' well-being. Because of the various chemicals added to our tap water, rain water is recommended by some breeders.

Green Food
Green Food in the form of wild seeding plants should be supplied in large and frequent quantities. Care must be taken to avoid any plants which may have been contaminated in any way, as these can prove lethal to all birds.

Chapter 10

Breeding –
Twites and Linnets

Pairing

Like many finches, linnets and twites pair up while they are in the winter flocks. For this reason it is best to pair them up early in the year so that they come into breeding condition together and will settle down better and more quickly when put into their breeding enclosure in the spring.

Nesting

Both species are timid, so reasonable cover as described in the previous chapter is essential for successful breeding. Supply fine twigs, dead grass, and plant down. These materials should be placed in the flight damp or where they will get wet, but clear of the perches so that they are not fouled. As previously stated, these species do not like interference, so it is best to watch from a distance to see where and when they are building their nest.

Brooding

As soon as the clutch is complete the hen will start sitting, the cock collecting food and returning about every half-hour to feed her by regurgitation. There are usually five eggs to a clutch. The hen will only leave the nest for short periods, to feed, drink, perhaps bathe, and defecate. The eggs hatch in 12 to 13 days.

Rearing

Like all seed-eaters, the young are fed partly on small insects for the first few days and then weaned onto half-ripe seeds. The food is collected by the cock and fed to the hen, who feeds the young by regurgitation. Until the young have developed and are beginning to feather the hen will only leave the nest for very short periods unless she is disturbed. Gradually, the cock is allowed to help to feed the young. It is most important to supply all the seeding weeds which can be collected during this period, plus soaked seed, eggfood and mealworms. The hen cleans out the nest for six or seven days. She then ceases to brood during the day and both parents collect food and feed the young directly by regurgitation.

Young linnets and twites develop very quickly and, because they are a heavily predated species, the young leave the nest before they can fly and hide separately in the under-

Linnet hen

growth, where the parents find them and continue to feed them. This is nature's way of ensuring that at least some survive. Any time after the eleventh day the youngsters will explode out of the nest if you disturb or even look at them. Do not try to put them back in the nest because they will only jump out again. As long as there is dry cover for them to hide in they will be all right. You will eventually find them flying round the flight about a week later. The cock goes on feeding them for about another week, until they are self-supporting.

Moult

Between July and September the adults moult, the hen looking the same after the moult but the cock linnet losing his breeding colour so that he looks similar to the hen. The red rump of the cock twite also fades, so that the cock and hen look similar. Early rounds of young moult at about twelve weeks, but late-bred young can moult as early as five weeks of age.

Colour Feeding

Twites and linnets are generally given the usual colour foods to enhance and deepen their colour. Most breeders use Carophyll Red*, which tends to bring a pink flush on the breast of the cock linnet and the rump of the cock twite. This certainly helps in sexing them.

* Registered trademark of Roche Products Limited

Ringing

The redpoll (lesser and mealy), twite and linnet are on Schedule 3 Part 1 of the Wild Life and Countryside Act 1981. For this reason, although it is permissible to keep them if they are not ringed, it is illegal to buy, sell or exhibit unringed specimens. Unfortunately, the Greenland redpoll *(rostrata)* and the Arctic redpoll *(hornemanni)* are not covered by Schedule 3, and may only be exhibited or sold under licence issued by the Department of the Environment.

There are two approved legal rings:

- The British Bird Council ring, which is exclusive to the British Bird fancy.
- The IOA ring, which is used for different types of birds and by exhibitors who may wish to send their birds to shows abroad. At present, quarantine and import/export regulations make exhibiting abroad very difficult. However, closer ties with Europe could see some beneficial changes in the regulations in the near future.

The British Bird Council ring is brown, and the letters 'BC' are stamped across it, followed by a size letter and serial number. Since 1991 rings also carry a year date. A great deal of work has been done over the years to find the best size for each species, and for the species under discussion these are as follows:

- Lesser redpoll and twite: code size B
- Mealy redpoll and linnet: code size C

The ring has to be put on the young bird while it is still in the nest, and is acceptable to the authorities as proof that the bird is aviary-bred.

One problem with the closed ring is that some birds resent either the interference in the nest or the foreign object on the chicks. For this reason, the parent birds must be accustomed to the owner and, if possible, reasonably tame before the breeding season. When the chick is ringed will depend on its rate of growth and the breeder's experience. Rings can usually be fitted to redpolls at five to six days of age, though it may be found necessary to ring the young of some large races of redpoll earlier, sometimes as early as three to four days. Fortunately, redpolls generally seem to tolerate the ringing of their young. However, twites and linnets have nervous dispositions, so ringing is best left as late as possible. With care they can usually be ringed at six days with few problems. The later ringing takes place, the less are the

Teasel

chances of rejection. This is because the hen no longer needs to remove the faecal sacs from the nest once the chicks start to void their faeces over the side of the nest, so she is no longer so meticulous in cleaning the nest out.

Rings that are fitted too early come off in the nest and are lost. If the ring can be removed easily after fitting it is best to leave it for a further day or two. This can arise particularly when the growth of chicks is staggered because they have hatched on different days. There are usually fewer problems with owner-bred hens than with bought-in stock. With newly-purchased hens it is best to be cautious and ring only the largest chick in the nest to begin with. If this is not mutilated or rejected, it is usually safe to ring the rest of the chicks. However, if all is not well, do not attempt to ring the remaining chicks under this hen. These chicks will either have to be left un-ringed or fostered out to a more reliable hen. Many breeders keep a few pairs of canaries to act as foster parents in such cases.

The actual time of day chosen to ring chicks will depend on the breeder's own circumstances. Some breeders like to ring towards dusk in the belief that the hen will settle down on the ringed chicks. However, if she is going to reject them, she will undoubtedly do so when cleaning the nest the following morning. For this reason, some breeders like to ring in the early morning so that a watch can be kept on the hen. If she rejects, the chicks can be picked up before they expire and either put back with their rings removed or fostered out. If a hen accepts her chicks being ringed, it really makes little difference what time of day you ring them. However, it is sensible to provide some rearing food or favourite seeding weeds to keep the hen busy while you ring the chicks.

For the inexperienced breeder, who will undoubtedly take some time to complete the ringing operation, it is best to leave one chick in the nest. The remainder can be removed and placed in a lined canary nest pan or something similar. Leaving one chick in the nest prevents the hen from being concerned if she returns before ringing is completed. Do not expect to ring chicks easily the first time that you try. It takes practice and experience to become proficient at the task. Many breeders find it necessary to ring the birds before they are seven days old, but they should be aware of the problems. It is well worth practising on canaries and budgerigars, which are much more tolerant of interference.

The recommended method for ringing is as follows (see illustrations below):

Fig 1   Fig 2   Fig 3   Fig 4   Fig 5

Ringing young birds

Redpoll x greenfinch hybrid cock

- As you look at the rings you will see that they are tapered slightly (caused by stamping the number on them). Always place the big end on first.
- It is essential to get the three long toes straight and parallel to each other. If the toes are crossed the ring will not go on. Sometimes it takes several goes to get the ring in this position (fig 1) because the young bird continually tries to clench its toes.
- A gentle pressure and slight twisting motion will now take the ring up over the ball of the foot (figs 2 and 3).
- The ring is then slid up the shank of the leg until the hind claw is released (figs 4 and 5).

Do not try to rush the job; it requires care and patience.

Exhibition

The most important rule if you are to be successful on the show bench is to ensure that your birds have access to water for regular bathing. Some birds are reluctant to bathe, but most follow suit when they see or hear other birds doing so. If they will not, or do not have access to bathing facilities, they should be sprayed regularly. Many successful exhibitors spray their birds if necessary, but prefer a bird to bathe naturally. When a bird bathes, it relaxes, allowing the water to penetrate the feather; when sprayed, it behaves as if it is trying to avoid the water, 'tightening up'. Birds soon accept spraying, however, and many look forward to and enjoy it. Without any doubt, rain water is best for their plumage. This is what wild birds use and they always carry a 'sheen' or gloss on the feather, obtained by bathing frequently.

A bird should get used to its show cage before it is exhibited. Some birds take to a show cage 'like a duck to water' as the saying goes, but others do not like to be confined. Such birds should be run into show cages for very short periods initially; eventually they will get accustomed to them. Occasionally one does meet a problem bird, but it is surprising how it will accept a show cage in time. Very often a bird, when shown at a small show for a few hours, gains confidence. Once acquired, it is never lost.

Some birds – just a few – have a nasty habit of facing the back of the cage. Such birds are known as 'back runners' and seldom overcome the habit. They are best left in the breeding pens. The ideal exhibition bird always faces the front of the cage. Redpolls are relatively easy to train and will usually settle down after a few sessions in a show cage. Some mealy redpolls develop the nasty habit of 'twirling', a wry movement of the neck that can be very difficult to cure and that is thought by some to be hereditary. Strangely, lesser redpolls rarely suffer this trait. Twites are active birds because of their nervous dispositions. However, with a little patience, they will usually learn to use a show cage correctly. Linnets, on the other hand, require a great deal of patience if they are to be trained to advantage. The main need is to train them to work the perches facing the front. Some allowance has to be made for movement as they are naturally active birds. Breeders usually find that the best show birds are 'born steady', as they say: 'a kind bird'.

Redpoll x bullfinch hybrid cock

When dealing with current-year birds, you should limit their training to short periods at first, returning them immediately after each session to their normal living quarters. Young birds are much more vulnerable to stress than adults, and losses will be experienced if they are put under too much stress too early in their lives. Never be in too much of a hurry to steady down that promising youngster. Patience is the key if you want to avoid disappointments.

The staging or presentation of British seed-eaters, mules and hybrids is very important if the exhibitor is to be successful. There is a slight difference in the sizes of show cages advocated by the Scottish British Bird and Mule Club, but we are all agreed that green is the acceptable colour for interiors and black for exteriors.

It is very important that exhibits are staged in the sizes advocated for the particular species. It is always permissible to use a larger cage but never a smaller one. Please remember that the sizes recommended and adopted are the minimum sizes and usually the most suitable.

It is most important that show cages are made by skilled cage makers who specialise in this particular job. It is also very important that internal and external decoration of the show cage is of the highest standard. Sometimes we see show cages that are poorly constructed and decorated. A good bird deserves a good cage; it certainly enhances a bird's chances on the show bench.

To maintain show cages in good condition it is important always to clean them after a show. Wash them thoroughly, particularly the perches, and place them in your carrying case ready for your next show. They also need repainting periodically. If a little polish is put on the cage prior to the show, cleaning with warm water is easy afterwards.

It must be pointed out to those just beginning to exhibit birds that the birds are only allowed to be kept in show cages for 72 hours and while being transported to and from the shows. Also, it is only permissible to confine a bird in a show cage for training for a maximum of one hour in any 24. At other times, the birds must be kept in their aviaries or in the recommended stock cages.

Show Cage
The correct show cage for redpolls, twites and linnets is No 2:

	Length	Height	Depth
English Pattern	28cm (11in)	24cm (9.5in)	11.5cm (4.5in)
Scottish Pattern	25cm (10in)	24cm (9.5in)	11.5cm (4.5in)

Gauge wires: No 14, set at 1.5cm (0.625in) centres.
Drinking hole: 2cm (0.75in) diameter
Bottom rail: 3.75 cm (1.5in) high
Top rail: (shaped) 2.5cm (1in) at the outside, sloping to 1.25cm (0.5in) at the centre.
Painted: Brolac Georgian Green inside, on the outside of the wires, on both top and bottom rails, and on the drinker. Glossy black outside top, bottom, back and sides.

Exhibition Standard - Lesser Redpoll
An exhibition lesser redpoll is a well-rounded, short, cobby bird, in colour a nice rich nutty-brown, with well-defined, plentiful lines on chest and flanks.
Size: Large as possible. 10 points
Type: Nicely-rounded full head of good width on short, thickset body, set well across the perch. 15 points
Colour and Markings: Rich nutty-brown throughout with plentiful well-defined flank workings, reasonably well-defined bib and crimson poll. When colour-fed, to show rich pink flush on breast and rump. Hen has more profuse working carried well into chest, lacks pink flush on breast. 50 points
Feather Quality and Condition: 10 points
Steadiness and Presentation: 15 points

Total: 100 points
Faults: Any tendency to grey-brown or mealy colour, lack of working, eye defects, deformities, poor presentation, insufficiently trained.
Notes: Buffs are of less intensive colour. Current-year birds are difficult to sex and carry profuse working and well-defined dark bib, lacking pink flush on breast and rump.

Exhibition Standard - Mealy Redpoll

An exhibition mealy is a well-rounded, cobby bird with a good width of head and a nice bib. Well-defined lines on chest and flanks.

Size: Large as possible. 10 points

Type: Full head of good width and rise set on a really thickset short body set well across the perch. 15 points

Colour and Markings: Rich grey brown with plentiful heavy, well-defined flank workings. Reasonably well-defined bib and crimson poll. When colour fed, to show rich pink flush on breast and rump. Hen has more profuse working carried well into chest, lacking pink flush on breast. 50 points

Feather Quality and Condition: 10 points

Steadiness and presentation: 15 points

Total: 100 points

Faults: Poor colour, lack of working, eye defects, deformities, poor presentation, insufficiently trained.

Notes: Buffs are of less intensive colour. Current-year birds are difficult to sex and carry profuse working and well-defined dark bib, lacking pink flush on breast and rump.

Exhibition Standard - Twite

The exhibition twite should be full-bodied and cobby, with neat, round and well-lined head; clear well-defined lines on chest and flanks, with well-defined whites in the wing and a good, rich, dark, nutty brown throughout.

Size: Large as possible. 10 points

Type: Nicely rounded full head, cobby well-filled body. 15 points

Colour and Markings: Rich dark nut brown throughout, distinctly lined on head and back, plentiful working on chest and flanks, well-defined whites in wings. 35 points

Feather Quality and Condition: 15 points

Steadiness and Presentation: 25 points

Total: 100 points

Faults: Poor colour, lack of working, eye defects, deformities, poor presentation, insufficiently trained.

Notes: Sexes similar, cocks plum colour on rump. Buffs of less intensive colour.

Exhibition Standard - Linnet

An exhibition linnet should be a nice cone shape with a well-rounded head, well-lined on top. Well-defined lines on throat under lower mandible and well-defined white edges to primaries. Fine even ticking and working on the chest and down the flanks.

Size: Large as possible. 15 points

Type: Nicely-rounded, full head, well-filled cone-shaped body of strong bold appearance. 15 points

Colour and Markings: Rich nutty brown throughout, distinct throat markings, well-defined, even working giving well-filled chest and carried well down the flanks. Well-defined whites in wings and tail. Hens darker brown, with plentiful heavy working on head, chest and flanks. Less distinct whites in wings and tail. 30 points

Feather Quality and Condition: 10 points

Steadiness and Presentation: 30 points

Total: 100

Faults: Poor colour, lack of working giving open-chest effect, eye defects, deformities, poor presentation, insufficiently trained.

Notes: Buffs of less intensive colour. Allowance should be made for natural movement. Even well-trained linnets have a tendency for more movement than many other species.

British Bird Colour Variant Standards

The following exhibition Standard of Points shall apply irrespective of species:

Type: As normal in all respects. 35 points

Colour and Markings: As Colour Standard for variety. 35 points

Size: As large as possible, but this only to take precedence when exhibits are considered of equal merit in regard to type and colour. 15 points

Condition and Presentation: Clean, steady, of good bloom, well presented. 15 points

Total: 100 points

Notes: Where yellow and buff exhibits are considered of equal merit, yellow to take precedence; however, where a buff of good rich colour is of superior type, buff to take precedence.

Faults: Poor type, bad wing carriage, eye defects, deformities, insufficiently trained, poor presentation.

Meadowsweet

Colour Standards

Lesser Redpoll, Cinnamon: A rich, ginger, cinnamon-brown, as evenly coloured as possible throughout. Poll cherry red. Breast flushed rose pink. The working, which should be profuse, and the bib tend to be obscured by the richness of body colour. Eyes light brown. Buffs, though being of slightly less intense colour, shall be given due consideration.

    Female – As above, but working a little more distinct. Lacks rose flush on breast.

    Faults – Patchy or washed-out colour, tendency to mealy redpoll colouring.

    Note – Current-year birds are difficult to sex, as cocks lack rose flush.

Mealy Redpoll, Cinnamon: A fawn shade of cinnamon brown, as evenly coloured as possible throughout. Poll bright crimson. Breast flushed rose pink. Distinct bib. Profuse, well-defined working. Eyes light brown. Buffs are of a slightly paler appearance, and shall be given due consideration.

    Female – As above, but working more profuse. Lacks rose flush on breast.

    Faults – Patchy or too dark a colour, obscuring working.

    Note – Current-year birds are difficult to sex as cocks lack rose flush.

Others: Colour standards for agate (silver) and Isabel redpolls have not as yet been drawn up but these colours, in both lesser and mealy redpolls, are currently under consideration.

Chapter 13

Mules and Hybrids

Mule is the fancier's term for offspring raised from a canary and a British finch; offspring from two British finches of different species are referred to as hybrids. Both types are really hybrids, and some show schedules refer to mules as canary hybrids. Mules and hybrids are bred for exhibition, song or ornamental purposes and are generally considered to be infertile. However, modern knowledge and the production of the red canary from the red-hooded siskin of South America suggest that some mules may be fertile when paired back to canaries, but perhaps not until they are two or three years old.

Good exhibition mules are produced from Norwich type canaries and sometimes from cross-breeds. The Norwich x Yorkshire cross has been used, and birds of a long-barrel type are preferred by some breeders. Best quality mules are generally obtained from jonque hens, either clear or lightly marked.

Both birds should be put together in a large cage or small aviary well before breeding condition is reached, by the beginning of January at the latest, to avoid any quarrelling. From then on they should be treated just like the other finches in your possession. If the first nest should prove infertile, remove the eggs, but leave the birds together and let them try again. When the young leave the nest, a clean nest pan should be introduced. About a fortnight later, when the young mules are feeding themselves, they should be removed and placed in a clean, large cage. They should be provided with plenty of egg food and water, together with soaked seed and green food.

The linnet, twite and redpoll regularly produce mules, numerically in that order. Linnets are used to produce both songster and exhibition mules. With these three finches it is normal practice to use the cock finch in the production of mules, but all produce mules in the reverse mating, and this is used especially in the production of the colour variant mules.

Hybrids are usually bred in small aviaries or larger cages, because they generally require more room than muling pairs. Any hybrids produced can be difficult to rear. Some pairs behave perfectly if supplied with all the natural food we can possibly gather while others, for various reasons, do not rear their young. Bullfinch hens are particularly tricky. In this case you could transfer the eggs to a reliable canary hen and leave her to rear those that hatch on the same diet as that on which she would rear her own young, with the addition of seeding weeds and grasses such as chickweed and dandelion. The greenfinch hen usually makes an excellent parent and can be left to hatch and rear her own eggs.

When young hybrids leave the nest they should not be removed from their parents until they are eating well for themselves. When weaned they should be provided with egg food, the usual seed mixture, natural food, and a shallow dish of water so that they can bathe.

Redpoll cocks have produced hybrids with the twite and linnet, and also with the greenfinch, goldfinch and siskin; reversed matings have also been successful. Redpoll cocks have produced hybrids with the hen bullfinch, hen chaffinch (less than six recorded to date) and hen brambling (only one recorded to date). Redpoll x crossbill would be one worth trying for.

Twite cocks have produced hybrids with the redpoll and linnet, as well as with the greenfinch, goldfinch and siskin, and again reverse matings have been successful. Others well worth trying for, none of which have been recorded in Great Britain to date, are twite x bullfinch, twite x chaffinch, twite x brambling and twite x crossbill.

Linnet cocks have produced hybrids when mated with redpolls, twites, greenfinches, goldfinches and siskin, and reverse matings have also produced. Linnet cocks readily hybridise with bullfinch hens. Other hens well worth trying them with would be chaffinch, brambling and crossbill.

You do not have to ring mules and hybrids, although you can if you wish. Whether ringed or not they can legally be bought, sold and exhibited, provided that both parents are listed on Schedule 3 Part 1 of the Wild Life and

Goldfinch x mealy redpoll hybrid cock

Countryside Act 1981. (The canary can be one parent provided that the other is on Schedule 3 Part 1.) At the time of writing this Act is under review. Hopefully any changes will be beneficial to this side of our hobby.

Exhibition birds should show clearly the characteristics of both parents and be of good size in relation to the species from which they are bred. They must have good colour. Mules and hybrids, other than some colour variants, are always colour fed for exhibition. They must be of nice cobby type and excel in quality and condition of feather.

Mutations & Colour Variants

It is not the intention of this book to delve too deeply into the world of genetics. However, some basic understanding of the genetic inheritance patterns of colour mutations is necessary if we are to control, improve and generally make the best use of these mutations.

There are three modes of inheritance: dominant, recessive sex-linked and recessive autosomal. If we were to look deeper within each of these groups we would find deviations such as incomplete dominants and full dominants, multiple alleles and deep recessives. If you wish to delve further into the subject you will find that many books have been published about it.

MUTATION INHERITANCE CHARTS

The following charts are for the guidance of those taking up the breeding of colour variants and can be applied to any species. However, they refer only to pairings involving the use of a single mutated colour form with that of pure normal, not to cross-colour pairing expeditions. The latter involve more than one colour form and are covered elsewhere.

Note

In the charts and pairing expectations used throughout, the cock is always listed first in the pairings and the following symbols are used:

/	denotes 'split', carrier of the mutation
-	when between two varieties, refers to a composite variety
SF	denotes single-factor dominant
DF	denotes double-factor dominant
=	denotes progeny expectations

Recessive, Sex-linked Mutation Chart
(referred to as **Sex-linked**)

Normal/Sex-linked	x	Normal	=	Normal Cocks, Normal/Sex-linked Cocks, Normal Hens, Sex-linked Hens
Normal	x	Sex-linked	=	Normal/Sex-linked Cocks, Normal Hens
Normal/sex-linked	x	Sex-linked	=	Normal/Sex-linked Cocks, Sex-linked Cocks, Normal Hens, Sex-linked Hens
Sex-linked	x	Normal	=	Normal/Sex-linked Cocks, Sex-linked Hens
Sex-linked	x	Sex-linked	=	Sex-linked Cocks, Sex-linked Hens

Recessive Autosomal Mutation Chart (referred to as **Recessive**)

Normal/Recessive	x	Normal	=	Normal Cocks, Normal/Recessive Cocks, Normal Hens, Normal/Recessive Hens

(Reverse Pairing gives same expectations)

Normal/Recessive	x	Normal/Recessive	=	Normal Cocks, Normal/Recessive Cocks, Recessive Cocks, Normal Hens, Normal/Recessive Hens, Recessive Hens
Recessive	x	Normal	=	Normal/Recessive Cocks, Normal/Recessive Hens

(Reverse Pairing gives same expectations)

Recessive	x	Normal/Recessive	=	Normal/RecessiveCocks, RecessiveCocks, Normal/Recessive Hens, Recessive Hens

(Reverse Pairing gives same expectations)

Recessive	x	Recessive	=	Recessive Cocks, Recessive Hens

Dominant Mutation Chart

Dominant (SF)	x	Normal	=	Normal Cocks, Dominant (SF) Cocks, Normal Hens, Dominant (SF) Hens

(Reverse Pairing gives same expectations)

Dominant (SF)	x	Dominant (SF)	=	Normal Cocks, Dominant (SF) Cocks, Dominant (DF) Cocks, Normal Hens, Dominant (SF) Hens, Dominant (DF) Hens
Dominant (SF)	x	Dominant (DF)	=	Dominant (SF) Cocks, Dominant (DF) Cocks, Dominant (SF) Hens, Dominant (DF) Hens

(Reverse Pairing gives same expectations)

Dominant (DF)	x	Normal	=	Dominant (SF) Cocks, Dominant (SF) Hens

(Reverse Pairing gives same expectations)

Dominant (DF)	x	Dominant (DF)	=	Dominant (DF) Cocks, Dominant (DF) Hens

Shepherd's purse

Plantain

SPONTANEOUS SPORTS

Mutated colour forms appear from time to time through spontaneous sports and, unless these are preserved by correct matings,
they can disappear as quickly as they came. Some understanding of
genetics will certainly increase our ability to perpetuate mutations
through these chance arrivals by enabling us to discover the mode
of inheritance. This is secondary to establishing the colour form and
follows through from the elimination of inheritance modes one at a
time.

Dominant Mutations

These are the easiest to establish, since a visual colour form of this
mutation is capable of producing its own likeness in the first generation, irrespective of its sex and without any inbreeding.

When you are breeding dominants the colour form is visual
and cannot be carried by a normal in hidden form (generally
known as a 'split' form). New colour forms that are dominant
mutations can turn up as spontaneous sports at any time, male or
female, but they are always in what is known as 'single-factor' form,
an incomplete dominant. As will be seen from the chart, when one
of these is paired to a normal, half of the progeny are of the
mutation colour. However, when two single factors of the mutation
are paired together they produce young of which 25% are of
normal colour and 75% of the mutated colour. Of the mutated
young, 25% will receive a double dose of the factor producing the
mutation (known as 'double-factor') and they may be visually
different (in a dilute factor, much paler) or appear the same.
Double-factor forms of the mutation are fully dominant and, when
paired to normals, produce all mutation young of the single-factor
type. So it will be seen that dominant mutations are not only the
easiest to establish but also lend themselves to improvements in
exhibition qualities when paired to good exhibition normals.

Recessive Sex-linked Mutations

These are not so easy to establish. Although the rules governing sex-
linked inheritance are quite straightforward it is important to
remember that the results from pairing a sex-linked cock of a
mutated colour form to a normal hen are quite different from those
obtained from pairing a normal-coloured cock to a sex-linked
mutation hen. The reason for this is that a cock can be pure normal,
a visual normal bird with the ability to pass on the colour mutation
to some of his young (referred to as a 'carrier' or 'split'), or of a
visual-mutated colour form; whereas a hen can only be a normal-
coloured bird or a visual colour mutation. In other words, a normal-

coloured hen cannot be split for the sex-linked mutation; she is what you see. Unfortunately, there is no significant visual difference between a normal cock and a visual normal cock carrying the mutation factor, so its true genetic make-up can only be proven through test matings. However, as can be seen from the chart, certain matings produce visual normal cocks guaranteed to be carriers of the mutation.

When a sex-linked colour mutation turns up, the first bird of the mutated form is always a hen. If such a hen is paired to a normal-colour cock all the young produced, both cocks and hens, are of normal colour, but all the young cocks, although of normal appearance, carry the new colour. If these young cocks are paired to normal hens, 25% of the young produced will be of the mutation colour. Because of the mode of inheritance these will all be hens, and normal hens will also be produced. All the young cocks produced will be visual normals, half of them pure normal and the other half carriers of the mutation colour. These young cocks would need to be test-mated to find out which are carrying the mutated gene.

It follows that, to establish the new colour in the shortest possible time, we need to obtain a new-colour cock. To do this we must resort to inbreeding, pairing a new-colour hen to either her father or one of her sons: a practice which should not be taken too far because it can lead to infertility, dead-in-shell or deformed and weak chicks. Once the new-colour cock has been produced it can be paired to an unrelated normal hen. All the young hens of the pairing will then be of the mutated colour and all the young cocks will be of normal appearance but carrying the mutation. These are called 'carriers' or 'splits' and shown as 'normal/mutation' on the tables. When sufficient distantly-related cocks and hens of the new colour are produced they can be paired together to give a clutch in which all the young, cocks and hens, are of the mutated colour form.

Recessive Autosomal Mutations

Because of their mode of inheritance, these can be difficult to establish. Inbreeding is necessary at first to establish these colour forms, despite the hazards described above. Patience and perseverance are essential to see these colour forms fully established. It is important to remember that, unlike the dominants and sex-linked mutations, splits occur in both cocks and hens.

It is also important to realise that the mutation must be present in both parents before visual examples can be produced. Recessive mutations can be carried for many generations in hidden split form but, when two splits come together, the visual form of the mutation is produced. These can be either cocks or hens. You can then pair these back to the opposite-sex parent. Such a pairing produces more of the mutation in visual form and all the non-visual young produced are carriers of the mutation.

This method achieves results in the shortest possible time but, as already discussed, at the risk of producing weak and sickly mutation young. In the long term it would be better to outcross with the visual mutation by pairing it to one, two or more unrelated normals. This pairing, although not producing any visual forms of the mutation, does produce all young splits for the mutation. You can then pair these more distantly-related birds together, split x split, producing much stronger young of the mutated colour form and thus ensuring a better chance of the survival and establishment of the mutation.

REDPOLL COLOUR VARIANTS

Reports of redpoll, twite and linnet colour variants can be traced back many years but it is only comparatively recently that any serious attempts have been made to establish them. The first redpoll mutation to be established was the cinnamon, a sex-linked mutation, pink-eyed on hatching, but the eyes darken after a few days.

Although cinnamon lesser redpolls had been reported from time to time it was not until the early 1970s that more than one was reported in the same year. This was when the process of establishing the mutation began. Much of the work was carried out by Jim Warman of Bromsgrove, Bob Partridge, and their close associates, and it took almost a decade.

Agate (silver) lesser redpoll cock

The cinnamon lesser redpoll is a very attractive mutation. The very best examples exhibit a richness of colour akin to ginger, shining like well-oiled teak. To be successful on the show-bench a normal lesser redpoll must excel in colour and the striated markings known as 'working'. The cinnamon lesser is no different in this respect, but the sheer depth of cinnamon colouration makes the working difficult to discern, particularly in cocks. Removing the depth of colour to make the working more visible is unthinkable and would ultimately have a serious retrograde effect on the colour of lesser redpoll stocks.

Thoughts turned to the mealy redpoll, which lacks the depth of colour possessed by the lesser while possessing all the working. It was envisaged that transferring the cinnamon mutation of the lesser to the mealy would produce a light cinnamon-coloured bird showing all the working. Bob Partridge started on the programme of transferring the mutation in 1983.

It was known that all the races of redpoll are fertile with each other, so there would be no problems with fertility. The main concern was to prevent the hybrids from finding their way back into the lesser redpoll stock. To prevent this, each generation of young required for the programme would be paired direct to mealy redpolls. Any not required would be used with canaries or other finches for the production of non-fertile hybrids. The programme was to take five years and the results were exactly as envisaged. Fortunately, a number of top breeders saw the potential in these birds; the late Derek Oldknow of Barlborough, Jack Fletcher of Glossop, Jimmy Dearnley of Wigan, Ken Chappel of Manchester and some of their close associates all held top quality strains of exhibition mealy redpolls. It did not take them long to produce cinnamon mealy redpolls equal to, and even surpassing, the best normals.

The agate (silver) sex-linked lesser redpoll, a dark-eyed dilute, originated from the continent and must have been established there while the cinnamon was being established in Great Britain. Some Belgium breeders came over to purchase cinnamon redpolls, which did not exist on the continent at that time, offering exchanges of mutation stocks that were either scarce or non-existent here. Among those offered were agate (silver) redpolls, which were still very scarce and expensive even in Belgium. From the first youngsters bred from these imports it became obvious that the mutation had been established using the continental race of lesser redpoll. This was very evident in the young carrier (normal/agate) cocks, which lacked richness of colour although good-coloured normals had been paired to the agates. It was recognised that it would take some time to breed agate lessers with the depth of colour desirable in Great Britain. Care was also needed to prevent them from finding their way into good strains of normal lessers, where they would have a detrimental effect on the colour. Some breeders recognised that it would be easier to upgrade these agates to exhibition meal redpoll standard. Phil Shaw of Mansfield started a programme to do so, quickly followed by other breeders.

Having established the sex-linked cinnamon and sex-linked dilute, it was not long before a combination of the two was produced. Possibly the first in Great Britain were the Isabel lessers bred by Bob Partridge in 1992. The first Isabel mealies were bred by Ken Chappel in 1994. Other redpoll colour variants recorded in recent years but not yet established are albino, dark-eyed white, pied, red-eyed recessive cinnamon, opal (recessive silver), recessive dilute (slate) and black. The charts below give expectations from pairings of the three established redpoll colour variants.

Isabel lesser redpoll pair (Right: cock, Left: hen)

Table 1

Normal/Cinnamon	x	Normal	=	Normal Cocks, Normal/Cinnamon Cocks, Normal Hens, Cinnamon Hens
Normal	x	Cinnamon	=	Normal/Cinnamon Cocks, Normal Hens
Normal/Cinnamon	x	Cinnamon	=	Normal/Cinnamon Cocks, Cinnamon Cocks, Normal Hens, Cinnamon Hens
Cinnamon	x	Normal	=	Normal/Cinnamon Cocks, Cinnamon Hens
Cinnamon	x	Cinnamon	=	Cinnamon Cocks, Cinnamon hen

Table 2

Normal/Agate	x	Normal	=	Normal Cocks, Normal/Agate Cocks, Normal Hens, Agate Hens
Normal	x	Agate	=	Normal/Agate Cocks, Normal Hens
Normal/Agate	x	Agate	=	Normal/Agate Cocks, Agate Cocks, Normal Hens, Agate Hens
Agate	x	Normal	=	Normal/Agate Cocks, Agate Hens
Agate	x	Agate	=	Agate Cocks, Agate Hens

Chapter 14

Table 3

Normal/Cinnamon	x	Agate	=	Normal/Agate Cocks, Normal/Cinnamon/Agate Cocks, Normal Hens, Cinnamon Hens
Normal/Agate	x	Cinnamon	=	Normal/Cinnamon Cocks, Normal/Cinnamon/Agate Cocks, Normal Hens, Agate Hens
Cinnamon	x	Agate	=	Normal/Cinnamon/Agate Cocks, Cinnamon Hens
Agate	x	Cinnamon	=	Normal/Cinnamon/Agate Cocks, Agate Hens
Normal/Cinnamon/Agate	x	Normal	=	Normal Cocks, Normal/Cinnamon Cocks, Normal/Agate Cocks, Normal/Cinnamon/Agate Cocks, Normal Hens, Cinnamon Hens, Agate Hens, Isabel Hens
Normal/Cinnamon/Agate	x	Cinnamon	=	Normal/Cinnamon Cocks, Normal/Cinnamon/Agate Cocks, Cinnamon Cocks, Cinnamon/Agate Cocks, Normal Hens, Cinnamon Hens, Agate Hens, Isabel Hens
Normal/Cinnamon/Agate	x	Agate	=	Normal/Agate Cocks, Normal/Cinnamon/Agate Cocks, Agate Cocks, Agate/Cinnamon Cocks, Normal Hens, Cinnamon Hens, Agate Hens, Isabel Hens
Normal	x	Isabel	=	Normal/Isabel Cocks, Normal Hens
Normal/Cinnamon	x	Isabel	=	Normal/Isabel Cocks, Cinnamon/Isabel Cocks, Normal Hens, Cinnamon Hens
Normal/Agate	x	Isabel	=	Normal/Isabel Cocks, Agate/Isabel Cocks, Normal Hens, Agate Hens
Normal/Cinnamon/Agate	x	Isabel	=	Normal/Isabel Cocks, Cinnamon/Isabel Cocks, Agate/Isabel Cocks, Isabel Cocks, Normal Hens, Cinnamon Hens, Agate Hens, Isabel Hens
Normal / Isabel	x	Isabel	=	Normal/Isabel Cocks, Cinnamon/Isabel Cocks, Agate/Isabel Cocks, Isabel Cocks, Normal Hens, Cinnamon Hens, Agate Hens, Isabel Hens
Cinnamon/Isabel	x	Isabel	=	Cinnamon/Isabel Cocks, Isabel Cocks, Cinnamon Hens, Isabel Hens
Agate/Isabel	x	Isabel	=	Agate/Isabel Cocks, Isabel Cocks, Agate Hens, Isabel Hens
Isabel	x	Normal	=	Normal/Isabel Cocks, Isabel Hens
Cinnamon	x	Isabel	=	Cinnamon/Isabel Cocks, Cinnamon Hens
Isabel	x	Cinnamon	=	Cinnamon/Isabel Cocks, Isabel Hens
Agate	x	Isabel	=	Agate/Isabel Cocks, Agate Hens
Isabel	x	Agate	=	Agate/Isabel Cocks, Isabel Hens
Isabel	x	Isabel	=	Isabel Cocks, Isabel Hens

TWITE AND LINNET COLOUR VARIANTS

Colour variants have been recorded in both twite and linnet, but reports of colour variant twites are particularly rare. Cinnamons, albinos, dark-eyed whites, pieds and dilute forms, including pheao, have all been reported but, as far as is known, none has been established either here or on the continent. No doubt in time colour forms will be established in both species.

Chapter 15

The Law

It is beyond the scope of this book to give a full explanation of the Wild Life and Countryside Act 1981, which is the current bird protection act; it is both long and complicated. All keepers and breeders of birds must make themselves fully acquainted with its provisions, and this applies especially to keepers and breeders of our native British Birds. Copies of the Act can be obtained from Her Majesty's Stationary Office. However, some of the most important points are as follows:

1   All wild birds, their nests and eggs are protected.

2   It is illegal to have any wild bird in your possession unless you have a special licence or permit to do so. A bird is only considered to be legally captive-bred if its parents were legally in captivity at the time that it was hatched in a cage or aviary. If you can prove that, the bird need not be ringed; but it is recommended that whenever possible all young birds are ringed.

3   It is illegal to buy or sell a native bird except by special licence unless it is listed only on Schedule 3 Part 1 of the Wild Life and Countryside Act 1981, and then again provided that it is correctly ringed with an approved ring of the correct size. (The lesser and mealy redpoll, the twite and the linnet are so listed; unfortunately, the Greenland and Arctic redpoll are not.)

4   Except under special licence, only birds listed on Schedule 3 Part 1 can be exhibited, and again they must be ringed with an approved ring of the correct size.

5   It is illegal to keep or confine any bird whatsoever in a cage that is not sufficient in height, length or breadth to permit the bird to stretch its wings freely except when:

(a) the bird is in the course of conveyance.

(b) the bird is undergoing treatment by a veterinary surgeon.

(c) the bird is being exhibited for competition. (However, it must not remain in a show cage for more than 72 hours.)

(d) the bird is being trained for exhibition. (However, it must not be so confined for more than one hour in any 24-hour period.)

Tribute

Sadly Peter Lander died before the series *Popular British Birds in Aviculture* could be published.

I first met Peter in the early 1960s when he approached me for some Siberian goldfinches. The goldfinch was a species for which he had a particular fondness.

In addition to keeping and breeding birds, Peter had a keen interest in all things ornithological. I found him a quiet, unassuming man who knew his own mind. He was the driving force behind the founding of The British Bird Council, and worked tirelessly on its behalf for many years. In recent years, by his own choice, he took a back seat, but was always there when needed to give advice and a helping hand.

I worked with Peter when he compiled *British Birds in Aviculture* for The British Bird Council and felt privileged when he asked me to be co-author of the *Popular British Birds in Aviculture* series. Without Peter's initiative this series would not have been produced.

A guiding light extinguished, but memories will light our way.

Bob Partridge